BRINKBURN PRIORY

NORTHUMBERLAND

Martin Roberts

D1798995

Brinkburn Priory lies in a secluded and enchanting setting, tucked away in woodland within a loop of the River Coquet. It was founded in the 1130s as a community of Augustinian canons, although the earliest surviving buildings date from the end of the twelfth century. Never a wealthy house, and frequently troubled by Scottish raids, it was one of the first monasteries to be closed at the Dissolution in 1536.

After the Dissolution the priory church was used for a while as the parish church, while parts of the monastic buildings were adapted to form a manor house. The condition of the church rapidly deteriorated, but after years of neglect it was carefully reroofed and restored in the mid-nineteenth century, and stands today as one of the finest examples of early Gothic architecture in Northumberland. The manor house was radically altered in the nineteenth century, and remained a family home until 1953.

This guidebook takes visitors on a tour of the whole site, and relates the history of the priory from its foundation to the present day.

❖ CONTENTS ❖

Brinkburn Priory, Longframlington, near Morpeth, Northumberland NE65 8AR
Visit our website at www.english-heritage.org.uk

Published by English Heritage
6th Floor, 100 Wood Street, London EC2V 7AN
© English Heritage 2003
First published by English Heritage 2003
Reprinted 2008, 2011, 2015, 2018

Unless otherwise stated, all photographs are © Historic England Archive and were taken by Keith Buck.
Photographs available from Historic England Archive, tel: 01793 414600
Editor: Katy Carter. Design: Hoop Design. Plan: Richard Morris.
Picture research: Diana Phillips.

Printed in England by Park Communications Ltd.
ISBN 978 1 85074 848 9
C50 03/18 04154

TOUR OF THE PRIORY

The visitor's first view of Brinkburn is the north doorway of the priory church, the framed focal point for the descent through the woods. In medieval times this was the main entrance to the church for the local people, who used the nave as their parish church. This doorway is characteristic of the Transitional style of architecture, the style in which Brinkburn Priory is almost wholly designed (see page 4).

THE CHURCH INTERIOR

North Doorway

The north doorway is an extraordinary and extreme example of Transitional building in the way it uses both Norman and Early English styles. It incorporates a very backward-looking doorway of Norman decoration comprising a series of three recessed semicircular arches: the innermost uses beakhead ornament – a row of bird and beast heads; and the outer two have chevron, or zigzag, mouldings. Above this is an entirely up-to-the-minute Early English arcade of three pointed arches with elegant trefoil heads. All the vertical edges of this

doorway have then been trimmed, as if with pinking shears, in fashionable dogtooth ornament.

Overview

The north doorway leads into the west end of the nave. The view of the whole church from here is very impressive and worth a moment's contemplation. The church comprises, from the east, an aisle-less presbytery where the high altar stands; north and south transepts, each with an eastern aisle of two small chapels; the central crossing, which supports the tower; and a nave with a north aisle only, a feature common in Augustinian churches.

The building of the church was begun in the final decades of the twelfth century. Traditionally churches are built from east to west but, at Brinkburn, the specific progress of the building work from one part of the church to the next has always confused scholars. The earliest work may be on the south side of the nave and transept while the west front, a more fully Gothic design, may mark the completion of the building in the early

The north entrance of the church, showing the Norman decoration of the doorway with the Early English arcade above

Right: This view of the church looking east reveals the simple and dignified proportions of the interior. The whole internal space is surprisingly grand in scale for such a modestly sized church, an impression enhanced by the very limited use of decoration

decades of the thirteenth century.

The open vista of the church from west end to east end is very much a modern view. It would not have been like this in medieval times. The canons would have occupied the east end of the church as far as the crossing; beneath this would have been their choir stalls, closed off from the nave to the west by a stone or timber screen called the pulpitum. In front of this, further west, was a passageway between the pulpitum and another screen, the rood screen, carrying above it a cross or rood. Marks in the masonry in this part of the church indicate the position of these screens.

The rood screen was the focal point for the lay members of the monastery (those who were not canons) and the local population who worshipped together in the nave where you are standing. Around you, in medieval times, the walls would have been plastered and, in parts, decorated with colourful wall paintings. The space would have been bare, as now; there were no pews for worshippers.

❖ TRANSITIONAL ARCHITECTURE ❖

In the last decades of the twelfth and the early decades of the thirteenth century, architecture in Britain was changing. It moved from the round-arched solidity of the Romanesque style, known as Norman in this country, to the more delicate pointed-arched buildings of the Gothic style, the first phase of which is called Early English.

This change was not uniformly smooth and many buildings which adopted new Gothic forms and decoration also clung to aspects of the familiar Norman style.

Left: The tower and east end of the church. Notice the keel moulding on the central shafts of the columns

Intermixed round and pointed arches are the most frequent example of this.

The Transitional style in the north of England is characterised firstly by the introduction of new decorative mouldings such as waterleaf capitals, often accompanied by column shafts shaped in cross section like the keel of a boat. Windows are long and narrow, and increasingly they have pointed heads. They are often seen in gable walls, divided by strongly modelled buttresses, and arranged in tiers reflecting the internal horizontal divisions of the church. The east end of Brinkburn church is a characteristically northern Transitional composition.

for vaulting ribs – on the backs of several capitals (the column heads) and on the aisle wall. This work may never have been completed.

Central Tower and Transepts

Walk up the central aisle until you are beneath the tower.

The piers supporting the central tower have three shafts on each face, the central one of which is keel moulded (see page 4). In the transepts, all these pier shafts descend to the ground, but towards the presbytery and nave they are cut short, to allow the canons' choir stalls to be fitted below.

Each transept has two chapels in its

The arcades of the nave, with the triforium (gallery) and windows above. These three levels of openings vary in shape, and unusually the openings of the triforium lie above the piers (columns), rather than the arches

Right: The northernmost chapel. The window has an ogee head – a double curve design – characteristic of the mid-fourteenth century

Nave and North Aisle

The nave and aisle are of six bays in length, with the lofty height divided between the arcade arches on the ground, the arcaded gallery or triforium above and clerestory windows at the top, which light the nave above the abutting aisle and cloister.

The original plan must have been for the north aisle to be vaulted, judging by the springers – the bases

ENGLISH HERITAGE / JONATHAN BAILEY

Presbytery

The climax of the church interior, architecturally and liturgically, is the east end of the presbytery, where the high altar stands and where the mass was celebrated. This is still the finest part of the building, a beautifully proportioned space, lit principally by three tiers of triple lancet windows.

In the north wall is a blocked shouldered or Caernarfon arch of early fourteenth-century date which gave access to a small room – perhaps a sacristy, where vessels and vestments were kept – and also to a spiral staircase. This room was removed during the restoration of the church. At the same time, in the south transept, a squint was uncovered. This narrow oblique opening, high in the triforium wall, may have allowed a view of the high altar for the canons coming down from their dormitory. The canons entered the church from this room via a doorway in the south transept for the night-time services. The night stairs, probably of timber, were located in the south-west corner and the blocked doorway is still visible in the wall here. The stone night stairs of the much larger Augustinian priory at Hexham still survive, probably the best example in the country.

On the north side of the presbytery lies the tomb slab of William, Prior of Brinkburn (d. 1484). The floor tiles here and throughout the church are copies of original ones found during the restoration, some of which were reset around the high altar.

Left: The Risen Christ *by Fenwick Lawson (b. 1932). This large beechwood sculpture hangs on the wall of the north transept. Its stark character successfully echoes the austerity of the church*

In the south wall of the presbytery is this double-arched recess containing a piscina and a credence – a small shelf where the canons would have placed the sacraments during the mass

eastern aisle. These chapels reflect the increasing requirement for additional altars, as the ritual of the church services grew more complex. They would have been dedicated to specific saints, almost certainly including the Virgin Mary. The canons would normally use them for individual celebration of the mass. The chapels were divided from each other by wooden screens: the marks where they were fixed on the walls still remain. Each of the chapels has a rib-vault – a stone roof consisting of two diagonal arches. The southernmost chapel in the south transept has a piscina – a stone basin and niche where the communion vessels were washed. Its basin appears to have been added later.

The door in the wall of the north transept beneath the wooden sculpture leads to stairs up to the bell turret and the bells, donated by Sir William Armstrong of nearby Cragside, a Tyneside industrialist, in 1866.

Furnishings and Stained-glass Windows

The furnishings in the church date from after the completion of the building restoration work, in the last quarter of the nineteenth century (see page 22). The timber pulpit of 1874 stands on a stone base with Frosterley marble columns. The high altar of 1898 is a memorial to Cadogan Hodgson Cadogan who restored the church. The altar supports are based on work in a number of Durham churches. The choir stalls and desks are Early English in style, while the sedilia, where the nineteenth-century clergy sat, is designed in the later Perpendicular style, and may not have been made for Brinkburn. In the southernmost chapel, an old altar slab with five consecration crosses stands on inverted columns. A similar slab, which may be original to Brinkburn, survives in one of the north transept chapels. The presbytery also contains the graves of seventeenth- and eighteenth-century parishioners as well as the grave slab of Cadogan Hodgson Cadogan (1888).

The organ of 1868 was built by William Hill, perhaps the most significant English organ builder of the century, and

This set of Victorian altar cross and candlesticks, though no longer at the priory, was designed for the high altar at Brinkburn

remains a fine unaltered example of his work. It was the gift of Sir William Armstrong of Cragside.

The stained glass in the church dates from the nineteenth-century restoration. William Wales, the great Newcastle manufacturer, installed many of the windows in the nave, aisles and transepts from 1864 onwards, notably the south transept gable. Grisaille glazing (plain coloured glass) has been fitted in some windows in imitation of the form of glazing known to have lit the medieval church.

MONASTIC BUILDINGS

Leave the church by the south transept door.

You will quickly see that there are very few remains of the monastic buildings that once abutted the church. The original priory would have had a quadrangle, or cloister, south of the nave surrounded by roofed passageways that connected the church to the domestic accommodation on the other three sides. The positions of those on the north, east and west sides are marked by modern paving and by the partial restoration of the cloister alley roof.

On the east side of the priory cloister would have been the chapter house, where the canons met daily to discuss business, with the dormitory on the floor above. On the south side would have been the buildings for the preparation and consumption of food, the kitchen and refectory, and on the

west side, if one was ever built at Brinkburn, there would probably have been storage facilities on the ground floor with perhaps the prior's accommodation above. Most of these buildings have been swept away, but remnants of the east range, probably the chapter house, survive, and significant parts of the refectory can be seen embedded in the later manor house (see below).

Three round-headed doorways lead from the church into the cloisters, all with varying architectural details. The transept door has waterleaf capitals, a characteristic design of the late twelfth century. The adjacent east nave door looks further backwards with old-fashioned Norman-style capitals, while the restored west nave door has more refined bell-shaped capitals and dogtooth ornament typical of the early thirteenth century.

In the west wall of the south transept is a double book cupboard. At the end

A reconstruction by Peter Dunn of Lanercost Priory, an Augustinian house of similar size to Brinkburn. This gives an impression of how the buildings around the cloister might have looked at Brinkburn

Left: The remains of the chapter house vestibule

The east nave door from the cloister is Norman in style

above the lancets was rebuilt during the nineteenth-century restoration and the wheel window is a design based on the suggestion of Cadogan Hodgson Cadogan, the owner, rather than any surviving evidence.

THE CHURCH EXTERIOR

Move eastwards, and look at the angle between the presbytery (east end) and south transept.

The small stone figure in a niche here is thought to have been inserted in the sixteenth century.

Walk further east, and turn to admire the east end of the church, architecturally the most composed and powerful part of Brinkburn. Then walk to the far end of the grass terrace, part of the landscaping surrounding the nineteenth-century manor house. The tunnel to the left is of unknown date, and is probably a garden folly.

Between the two doors in the south wall of the church is this beautiful pointed and trefoiled wall arcade, originally supported on shafts detached from the wall

of the south transept is a vaulted room which may have been a passageway, but is more likely to have been a vestibule under the dormitory, leading to the loftier space of the chapter house beyond.

Walk further south and look back at the south transept wall.

High in the wall you can see the blocked doorway for the night stairs to the church and the corbels – projecting stone blocks – that supported the roof timbers of the dormitory. This must have been an unusual roof form that did not directly abut the transept, as the depth of the tall lancet windows and the absence of gabled roof marks indicate. The gable

Right: The south transept wall. Notice the blocked doorway on the right for the night stairs to the church

Beyond the terrace is the private mill house, site of one of the gateways to the priory precinct. Turn to enjoy the finest of Brinkburn's many viewpoints. This view of the church and manor house is a superb composition, blending true Gothic and Gothic Revival in balanced and complementary forms.

Pass the church on its north (right) side, past the north doorway again, to the west front.

This is an assured composition, and a fully developed Early English design of the early thirteenth century. The south-west corner was the one part of the original church completely

The church from the south-east. The tiered lancets of the east façade are divided by shallow buttresses that change their shape at each level, first square, then semi-octagonal, then keel-shaped, and finally fading into the gable with a conical top – one of the church's most delightful details

The west front of the church

Right: The south-west angle of the church in the 1850s, before restoration. The turret on the left contained a spiral staircase that gave access to a passage across the west front. This was lost during the restoration when this corner was replaced in solid masonry and the passageway blocked

The conversion of the monastic buildings into a new house followed quickly after the closure of the priory in 1536. That new but rambling house with its medieval core was radically altered twice in the nineteenth century (*c*.1810–11 and 1830–37), fortunately retaining a substantial part of the monastic refectory. A walk around the outside of the house will help orientate you before you go inside.

Exterior

Externally the building is very much of two halves. The wing to the east dates from 1810–11 and was the work of the new owner, Richard Hodgson.

destroyed before the restoration, and in rebuilding it Cadogan and his architect, Austin, were careful to reconstruct modestly, at some cost to the symmetry of the elevation.

THE MANOR HOUSE

The present poor condition of the manor house interior is the result of extensive dry rot that nearly destroyed the building in the 1950s. Wooden plugs in the walls reveal where damaged panelling was stripped away. The ground floor and basement levels may be visited at present, but much remains incomplete, awaiting full restoration.

It incorporates the south range of the monastic buildings and when built must have improved the principal reception rooms in the earlier house, with a new drawing room, dining room and library as well as providing additional bedrooms. It was built of rubble stonework, which would have been rendered in stucco – smooth plasterwork – in the fashion of the time. An exception was the central semicircular bay, projecting eastwards, which was built in square blocked stone (ashlar), reflecting the stonework of the neighbouring church.

Twenty years later the centre and west end of the old house were demolished and rebuilt by Richard Hodgson's son William to provide more reception rooms and bedrooms, and greatly improved service accommodation (1830–37). John Dobson was the architect and he designed a picturesque building of variable height, culminating in a towered porch, a composition not unlike the building he had demolished. The external treatment was Tudor Gothic in style and exposed stonework was now fashionable. So Dobson's walls are roughly chiselled, or dressed, to give an appearance of instant maturity that would sit happily beside the weathered walls of the priory church. He stripped the stucco off Hodgson's east end to match the rest and blocked one of the two remaining double-storey windows in its north wall, to provide a fireplace for a small room on the first-floor landing.

The north façade of the manor house

The blocked-up recess for the canons' lavatorium, where they washed before meals

One of the windows from the first house created after the Dissolution

Right: The surviving basement of the refectory

Interior

Enter the house by the main porch.

The whole of the ground floor is supported on a basement that sits in the heavily sloping ground down to the river.

The entrance hall is Hodgson's work of *c.*1810–11 and is decorated in the same delicate Gothic manner as the exterior, with pretty plasterwork cornices. The lightness of this treatment is compromised by the gutted nature of the hall, part dry rot treatment, part archaeological 'unpicking' of the 1960s. The compensation for this current state is the very fortunate survival of the north wall of the twelfth-century refectory, the monks' dining hall, on the south side of the entrance hall facing you. It stands to its original height and most of its length, now fully exposed, and includes the blocked-up recess for the lavatorium inserted in the early thirteenth century. This was the communal washing trough used by the canons before meals. It was damaged by the later blocking and plastering of the walls. One of the blocked doorways to the west (right) of the lavatorium may represent the original entrance to the refectory.

The sixteenth- or early seventeenth-century mullioned (vertically divided) windows inserted into this wall are from the two-storey conversion work carried out after the Dissolution of the monastery. This was part of a more extensive range of buildings retained until Hodgson's work of around 1810–11.

The entrance hall gives access to the three principal reception rooms – from the west, the dining room, library and drawing room. The drawing room looks both south over the river and east along the lawned terrace. West of the entrance porch lie the gutted service rooms of the Dobson building.

Descend to the basement by the western stairs.

The kitchen and other service areas of the nineteenth-century house were located here. The basement of the refectory survives with a later inserted stone barrel vault, which probably dates from the conversion of the buildings after the Dissolution.

HISTORY OF THE PRIORY

❖

THE AUGUSTINIAN ORDER

By the second half of the eleventh century the concept of Christian monastic life – based on the two seemingly contradictory ideals of solitude and community – had existed for eight centuries. The sixth-century Rule of St Benedict – a series of directions for the life of a monastic community – had been adopted throughout mainland Europe, and in England too after 1066. But many reformers believed that the Benedictine communities had become lax and undisciplined, and new religious orders sought to re-establish the traditions of simplicity and purity that had first characterised St Benedict's Rule. Asceticism was the hallmark of the new orders, of which the Cistercians were the most important. All these communities of monks were bound by a common rule, sharing vows of poverty, chastity and obedience.

Unlike monks, priests undertook their religious duties within the wider world, serving the lay community. The priests who served the major churches and cathedrals, unrestrained by a religious rule, were known as Secular Canons. Efforts were made during the eleventh century to organise these canons into a collective monastic life sharing a common rule. This led to the establishment of the Regular Canons. One of the new orders of canons was the Augustinian order, which adopted the Rule of St Augustine of Hippo (354–430). This rule embraced the established monastic vows, but was flexible enough to include the Augustinian canons' role as priests tending to the spiritual needs of lay people. The Augustinians were known as the Black Canons from the colour of their clothing.

Augustinian communities, and therefore their monasteries, tended to be smaller and less expensive to maintain than those of the other orders. There were exceptions: notably, in the north of England, at Carlisle, Hexham and Guisborough. The first house of the order in

Left: The twelfth-century seal of Brinkburn Priory, depicting Saints Peter and Paul. (Drawing, from a cast in the British Museum, by Peter Forster)

Below: St Augustine of Hippo preaching to his disciples, from a twelfth-century English manuscript. The writings of this fifth-century bishop formed the basis for the Augustinian rule

Right: St John, a fourteenth-century prior of Bridlington, wearing the black habit of his order. Bridlington in Yorkshire was one of the most important Augustinian priories in northern England

Above: The tomb slab of a fourteenth-century priest at Felton Church. Felton was part of the original endowment of Brinkburn and this may well be part of a memorial to one of the priory's canons who served as a priest at Felton. (Photograph by permission of the vicar of St Michael and All Angels, Felton)

The mill at Brinkburn formed an important part of the monastic economy. This illustration is from the fourteenth-century Luttrell Psalter

England was that at St Botolph's at Colchester, Essex, founded in 1093.

FOUNDATION AT BRINKBURN

By the twelfth century the incoming Norman barons were settling and developing the lands given to them by the king, Henry I, a process largely complete by his death in 1135. It was common, almost fashionable, at this time, when the monastic revival was at its height, for these landowners to establish new monasteries within their recently acquired estates. The new orders were increasingly turning their backs on the towns and cities, seeking quieter rural communities.

William Bertram, lord of Mitford, founded a house for Augustinian canons at Brinkburn between the years 1130 and 1135. There probably would have been twelve canons at the foundation, a number only slightly exceeded during the life of the monastery. Ralph, the first prior, came from the monastery of St Mary de Insula, which was probably Pentney Priory in Norfolk.

The priory site would have offered the canons the seclusion they sought, with the adjacent River Coquet offering a good water supply and drainage. The land had been occupied long before: on the heugh, or headland, above the priory (beside the visitor car park) lies a large ditched enclosure which was probably an Iron Age settlement.

❖ LIFE AT THE PRIORY ❖

The daily life of the Augustinian canons was structured by the routine of seven services a day. Many of the smaller monasteries, like Brinkburn, with only a handful of canons, may well have relaxed this routine. The services for canons were shorter than those for monks, as they had other duties as priests to attend to.

The canons were woken for the first and longest service of the day, *Matins,* at around 2am, during which *Lauds,* in effect the second service, was held. The return to bed lasted until 6am when they again descended the night stairs into the church for *Prime,* a short service. This was followed by morning ablutions and a light breakfast taken standing in the refectory. The daily work of each canon then began. Some served as parish priests in churches belonging to the priory.

Black monks at prayer, from an early fifteenth-century psalter

BRITISH LIBRARY COTT. DOM. A XVII. FOL.122V

Others would have been employed in instruction for novices perhaps, or reading, study or writing. The more senior members oversaw the administration of the priory, its estates, farms and woodland. Lay servants and cooks would undertake the more menial duties.

Terce at about 9am was the celebration of the mass, and was followed by the daily meeting in the chapter house. During this meeting all the issues requiring collective discussion and decision were aired before the prior, after a reading by one of the canons from the chapters of their Rule. The next service in the church, at noon, was *Sext,* which, if *Terce* had not been held, would be a mass. Dinner followed in the refectory. This was the main meal of the day; afterwards the canons enjoyed a siesta until *Vespers* at 6pm. A light supper followed before *Compline* at 7pm, after which the canons retired to their dormitory for the night.

The new monastery at Brinkburn could not exist in isolation. William gave the canons a moderately sized estate of about 3500 acres on both sides of the River Coquet. This was supplemented by later gifts of land. Like many other communities at this time, the canons, directly or through their tenants, would have begun the task of clearance of forest and scrub and establishing new productive farmland or managed woodland. The rentals from their tenanted land, paid in cash or kind, provided a regular income to sustain the monastic community.

Their estate included land through-out Northumberland (pastures,

The building of an abbey church, from an early fourteenth-century manuscript

The seal of Robert Bruce, showing the king mounted on horseback

BRITISH LIBRARY MS ROYAL 14 E III, FOL. 85V

NATIONAL RECORDS OF SCOTLAND

woodland, arable, fisheries, saltpans and mills), urban holdings in Newcastle, a shop in Corbridge and isolated parcels of land in County Durham. The canons also derived benefit from the gift of churches as well as land. The church of Felton was granted by the founder, William Bertram I, and Longhorsley was added in the fourteenth century.

BUILDING THE MONASTERY

The earliest surviving priory buildings at Brinkburn date from the end of the twelfth century, not from the foundation of c.1130–1135. How did the young community live in those early years? What buildings did they construct? The written records are silent on this period and there have been no archaeological excavations that might have revealed earlier buildings.

Based on evidence elsewhere we have to assume that the canons of Brinkburn would have established a range of timber buildings, including at least a small chapel or church, probably of stone. Brinkburn's foundation charter suggests, unusually, that a chapel may well have existed on the site before their arrival. The canons would have added a dormitory, refectory and kitchen,

though even an infirmary is mentioned in the early documents.

THE SCOTTISH THREAT

If the daily routine of the canons of Brinkburn did not merit specific record, the surviving documents are equally silent about much of the priory's history. The little that remains speaks loudest of the monastery's poverty and its vulnerability to Scottish attack.

Edward I's conquest of Scotland in the early fourteenth century was followed by the accession of his weak son, Edward II, and the rise of the powerful Scottish king, Robert Bruce. In 1315, on one of his frequent incursions south, Bruce destroyed the monastery at Brinkburn, forcing the thirteen canons to flee and beg for food. The canons pleaded to Edward II for help, and seven years later again petitioned him for relief from their losses. In 1331 they sought a pardon from money owing to the crown 'as they are so utterly destroyed by the Scottish war'. Any return to normality that might have been expected to follow the total defeat of the Scots at the Battle of Neville's Cross in 1346 would have been shortlived. The Black Death followed in 1349, killing half the region's population. The priory lay within the diocese of Durham and further requests for help to the bishop in 1391 resulted in the gift of Longhorsley church with its valuable tithes. This was one of the last endowments the priory received.

LATER BUILDING WORK

After the church had been completed, early in the thirteenth century, we can assume that the next building campaign took place within the canons' accommodation around the cloister. First built in timber, these ranges were gradually replaced in stone. The refectory, already in stone by this time, was further improved with a new lavatorium (see page 14). Whether the infirmarer's chapel mentioned in 1253 was newly built of stone, or was a timber survivor from the early monastery, we do not know. But it demonstrates that the priory must have been a much larger complex of buildings in the thirteenth century than that which we see today.

During the fourteenth century one chamber was added over the north aisle of the church and another over the choir, using materials from a twelfth-century building. These rooms may have been a library or treasury for the priory's valuables. Their true function is unknown, but given the circumstances of the Scottish attacks, the documented destruction and the evident lack of funds, any new construction is remarkable. This work may represent the replacement of damaged buildings with new accommodation in a more secure and inaccessible position.

DECLINE AND DISSOLUTION

The Brinkburn archives for the fifteenth century are as bleak as those for the previous century. There are no contracts for new building works, no major endowments. Instead, after the cattle thefts in 1419, and sheep rustling in 1441, there follows a description of the priory in 1484 as 'plundered of its animals and other goods, and its possessions burned and wasted by the … Scots'.

Things did not improve in the early sixteenth century when the monastery was temporarily seized and one of its canons subsequently murdered. This canon was Sir Richard Lighton, who was killed in about 1521 'by the sword' by Humphry Lisle, supposedly because he was occupying land which the Lisles claimed to be theirs.

Beside these local difficulties, the future of the priory was increasingly influenced by the growing national crisis surrounding King Henry VIII. His divorce from Catherine of Aragon and marriage to Anne Boleyn led to a rift with the church in Rome and his own declaration as head of the church in England. An assessment of the wealth of the monasteries, called the *Valor Ecclesiasticus*, was carried out on his orders in 1535; Brinkburn, still an impoverished house, was valued at only £69. The following year, under the Act of Suppression, Brinkburn was closed along with all other monasteries with an income below £200. The six surviving canons were pensioned off and final payments were made to their servants and farm workers.

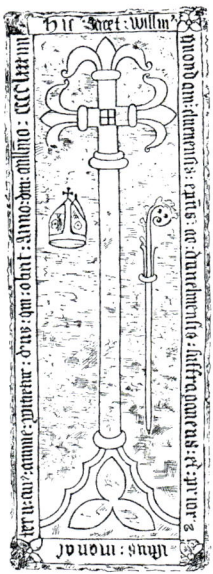

The tomb slab of William, a fifteenth-century prior of Brinkburn, in the presbytery

Henry VIII, depicted in an initial letter from the Valor Ecclesiasticus, *the valuation of all monastic property in 1535*

An engraving of Brinkburn from the south-west by the Buck brothers, dated 1728. It shows the ruined south-west corner of the nave (left) and the surviving chapter house (right). The manor house has been 'removed' by the artists to improve the view of the church

NATIONAL MONUMENTS RECORD

After the Dissolution

The priory site, complete with the water mill, 'tanne house' and a barn, were leased to Cuthbert Carnaby in 1536, along with substantial surrounding land. In the following decades the instability of the period is graphically illustrated by the number of times the priory lease and tenancy changed hands, often prompted by the demise of the holder. Twice, treason and beheading led to loss of the lease, in 1553 and 1572. In 1569 the tenancy was forfeited by participation in the Rising of the North – the attempt by some Catholic earls to unite the north in support of Mary, Queen of Scots.

The church and its bells were retained in use as a parish church, but by 1602 a visitation reported: 'the church is still in decaie in the roof and windows; they have no communion table and no surpcloth'. Apparently little or nothing was done to the building. Further lead was stolen off the roof in 1665 and by the end of the century the roof had collapsed and services had ceased.

As was common practice after the Dissolution, the undamaged monastic buildings were occupied as a private house. Although the monastic buildings were largely demolished, and the lead and stone sold, the refectory in the south range of the cloisters and 'the tower' are described as keeping their lead roofs after the first campaign of demolition was completed. The new

Brinkburn Priory in 1807, by Paul Sandby Munn. Viewed from the north-west, it illustrates part of the early manor house

house centred on the refectory and probably the buildings in the west range, which may have included 'the tower'. In 1626 the site was sold to George Fenwick, grandson of an earlier tenant, whose family held Brinkburn until 1792. They used the house at first as their main residence. But by 1747 the family had left it, and by 1769 it was described as 'in decay'.

The church meanwhile remained unroofed and also ruined. About the middle of the eighteenth century Dr Sharp, Archdeacon of Northumberland, attempted to have the church reroofed and the fabric repaired. In 1766 funds were made available, but legal difficulties prevented work from starting.

In 1792 the estate was sold to Joseph Hetherington for £20,500, and by descent through family inheritance, marriage and sale it transferred to the Hodgson, then Cadogan and finally the Fenwick family. By 1807 the house was in ruins and Joseph's brother, John Hetherington, is said to have begun repairs before his death in 1808 and the arrival of his son-in-law, the new owner Richard Hodgson, in 1810.

THE NINETEENTH-CENTURY RESTORATION

Richard Hodgson is credited with most or all of the new work on the eastern side of the manor house, completed in 1811. His architect is unknown, but the new work's unpretentious character and light Gothic manner suggest that it may have resulted solely from a collaboration between owner and builder.

Richard's son, Major William Hodgson, began work on a new phase of the manor house in 1830. He employed the fashionable and talented Newcastle architect John Dobson, who in 1831 demolished the older manor house built on the site of the west range of the monastery. Dobson designed the new building as a large picturesque Tudor Gothic pile, a style that he had begun to employ in a number of country house commissions from the late 1820s. The new work was completed in 1837. During the demolition of a wooden building near the north-west corner of the church in 1834, an important hoard of medieval gold coins was found in a large bronze pot beneath a hearthstone.

In the mid-nineteenth century the owner of Brinkburn, Cadogan

This sketch, now in Northumberland Record Office, is labelled 'the part of Brinkburn Priory house pulled down in 1831'. (Reproduced by kind permission of Mr H. A. P. Fenwick)

This sketch by J. M. W. Turner of Brinkburn from the south-east, dated c.1801, shows the ruined state of the manor house at that time

Hodgson Cadogan, revived the idea of restoring the church and chose as his architect Thomas Austin of Newcastle, who had taken over the practice of John Dobson. Austin and his later partner, R. J. Johnson, did a considerable amount of reputable church work in the county later in the century. Victorian restorations of medieval parish churches were increasingly common at the time, and archaeological research and considered restorations were often set aside for more inventive and newly designed work. Against this background, Austin's work is very restrained and generally respectful of the medieval fabric. Work began in 1858 and the building was enclosed the following year. The rebuilding of the missing south-west corner of the nave followed the original plan but, in the absence of certain knowledge of how the south-west turret looked, Austin showed commendable restraint by the standards of the time in not replicating the north-west turret. The greatest loss was that of the additional upper rooms over the choir and north aisle, and the complete removal of the sacristy.

The removal of the later additions enabled the new pine roof structure, of scissor-brace pattern, to follow the original high pitches of the thirteenth-century church.

THE LATER HOUSE AND GARDENS

The additions to the house designed by John Dobson in the 1830s gave the Cadogans, and later the Fenwicks, a country seat appropriate to their status in the middle gentry of Northumberland families. The surroundings of the manor house would have been cultivated even in monastic times, and by the time of Dobson's reworking of the house the landscaping would have been far more informal in character, to match the picturesque qualities of the new building.

The terracing to the east of the church was probably laid out for croquet and tennis after the completion of the church in 1860. In the late nineteenth century a rose garden was set out on the highest terrace, complete with stone obelisk and freestanding rose arches. The

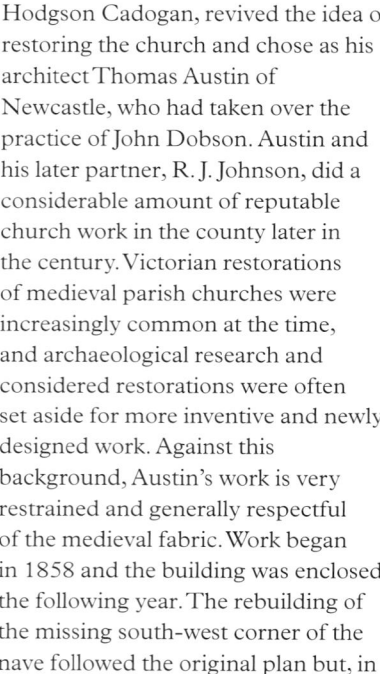

A design for the manor house by John Dobson, dated 1833. This shows the manor house with a west wing, intended for the historic Anderson Place staircase from Newcastle, but never built

a larger walled garden and hothouse were built on higher ground at the entrance to the estate by the roadside lodge.

The Fenwick family finally moved out of the manor house in 1953, and in 1962 the owner, H. A. Cadogan Fenwick, placed the buildings at Brinkburn in the guardianship of the then Ministry of Public Building and Works. They were opened to the public in 1965 and are now in the care of English Heritage. The Mill House is in the care of the Landmark Trust and is private property. The priory church is the home of the acclaimed annual Brinkburn Music Festival of classical music, held in July.

Left: This photograph, probably taken in the 1850s, shows a man drawing water from the millrace

enigmatic stone tunnel is probably a garden folly, no doubt invested with supposed mystical and monastic origins. Because the manor house stood in a cold and often sunless spot,

Captain and Mrs Lancelot Fenwick at Brinkburn in the 1930s. Captain Fenwick was the last person to live in the house

PRIVATE COLLECTION

The priory and manor house, seen from across the River Coquet

Further Reading

Visitors who want to learn more of Brinkburn's history would find the Northumberland County History Committee's *History of Northumberland* volume valuable. To understand Brinkburn's architecture in the context of the whole county, the best source would be the *Northumberland* volume of the Buildings of England series (second edition, Penguin, 1992) by Nikolaus Pevsner, John Grundy *et al.*

For a general view of monasteries within the wider medieval countryside, Mick Aston's *Monasteries in the Landscape* (second edition, Tempus, 2000) is recommended. *Medieval Religious Houses: England and Wales*, by Dom David Knowles and R. Neville Hadcock (1971), is a comprehensive account of the monastic establishment.

For those seeking more concealed treasures, Cadogan Hodgson Cadogan's own diary account of the restoration of the priory church, kept in Northumberland Record Office, is a fascinating read.

Acknowledgements

Three people deserve special thanks: David Sherlock for sharing his knowledge and archive on the site; Elfreda Hanby, whose researches and knowledge have been invaluable; and finally Katy Carter, the editor, who shaped, moulded and greatly improved the raw material for this guide.

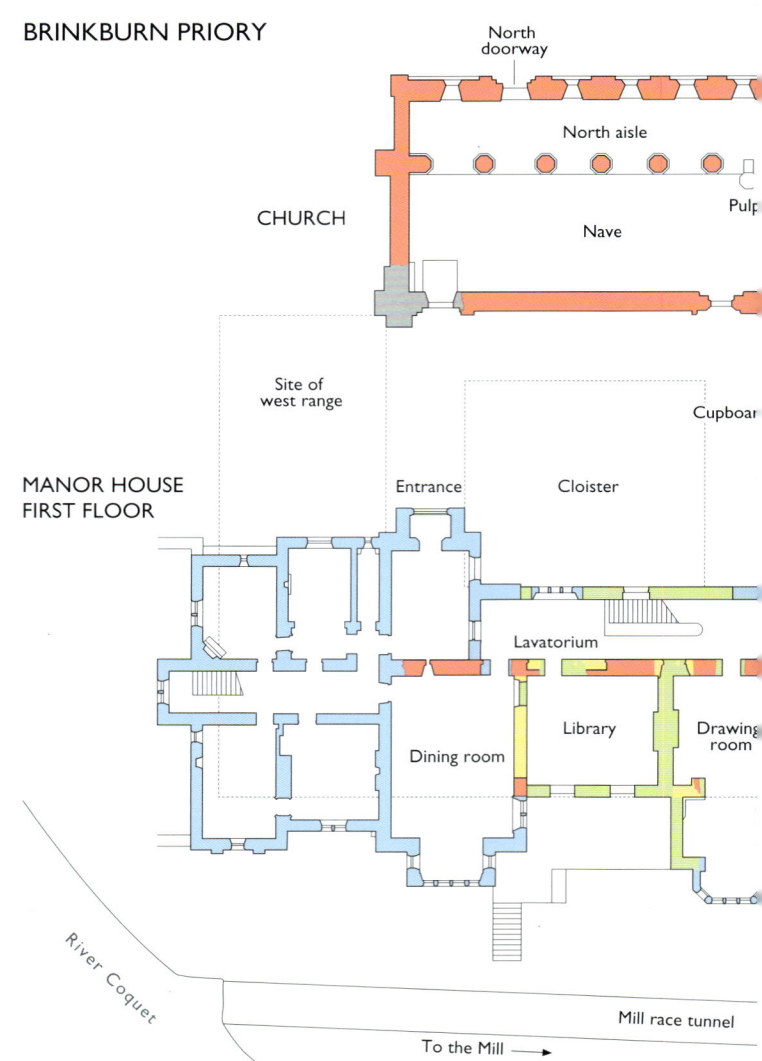

BRINKBURN PRIORY

CHURCH

MANOR HOUSE
FIRST FLOOR

North doorway

North aisle

Pulp

Nave

Site of west range

Cupboar

Entrance

Cloister

Lavatorium

Library

Drawing room

Dining room

River Coquet

Mill race tunnel

To the Mill ⟶